孔子学院总部 /
国家汉办汉语国际推广成都基地规划教材

走进天府系列教材【成都印象】

练武术

Practicing Martial Arts

西 南 财 经 大 学　著
汉语国际推广成都基地

西南财经大学出版社

中国·成都

西 南 财 经 大 学
汉语国际推广成都基地 著

总策划 涂文涛

策 划

李永强

主 编

梁 婷 白巧燕

编 者

《成都印象·游成都》 胡倩琳

《成都印象·居成都》 郑 莹

《成都印象·吃川菜》 谢 娟 王 新

《成都印象·品川茶》 肖 静

《成都印象·饮川酒》 谢 娟

《成都印象·看川剧》 郑 莹

《成都印象·绣蜀绣》 谢 娟

《成都印象·梦三国之蜀国》 蒋林益 胡佩迦

《成都印象·悟道教》 沙 莎 吕 彦 陈 茉

《成都印象·练武术》 邓 帆 刘 亚

审 订 冯卫东

英文翻译

Alexander Demmelhuber

Introduction

Practicing Martial Arts is one part of the "Impressions of Chengdu" textbook series promoted by the Chengdu Base of Confucius Institute Headquarters and published by the Southwestern University of Finance and Economics. This textbook was edited on the basis of the Confucius Institute Headquarters'/Hanban's "International Curriculum for Chinese Language Education" (hereinafter referred to as "Curriculum"). The vocabulary and grammar items found in levels 5 to 6 of the Curriculum are presented in narrative and dialog forms, making up eight lessons in total: the first four lessons mainly give an overview of martial arts from the perspectives of history, function, culture and schools; the fifth lesson is about"Martial Arts for International Students", mainly introducing several kinds of martial arts suitable for international students to practice. In the sixth lesson, "Tai Chi", the reader will learn what makes Tai Chi special, about its schools and other related facts as well as about its popularity in Chengdu. The title of Lesson Seven is "Tai Chi in the City of Hibiscus". In Lesson Eight, the reader is briefly introduced to some commonly used words related to martial arts in everyday life, in dialog form which makes the application of these terms more practicable and interesting. The appendix "Recommended Martial Arts Movies, Shows and Books" allows students to acquire a comprehensive understanding of Chinese martial arts from various angles: they will experience the influence of martial arts on people's lives while learning the basics of martials arts and also provides them with assistance in further understanding martial arts. This book will hopefully broaden the cultural horizon of intermediate and advanced students of Chinese and also improve their overall language proficiency.

Hopefully, you will enjoy *Practicing Martial Arts*, and we are looking forward to any criticism or suggestions you might have. Hanban gave us much help and support during editing of this book and we would like to take this opportunity to express our gratitude.

　　《练武术》是西南财经大学汉语国际推广成都基地推出的《成都印象》系列教材之一。教材以孔子学院总部/国家汉办的《国际汉语教学通用课程大纲》为基本编写依据，并以该大纲中的 5-6 级词汇和语法项目为主，采用叙述和对话两种表现形式，共八课：前四课主要从历史、作用、文化与派别的角度对武术进行简单介绍；第五课为"留学生练武术"，主要介绍几种适合留学生练习的武术；第六、七课分别介绍了太极拳的特点、流派等相关知识以及在成都地区的普及情况；第八课为"生活中的武术用语"，以对话形式，简单介绍生活中常用的、与武术有关的词语，增加实用性和趣味性；文后附录"武术影视、书籍推介"，可帮助留学生多角度、全面了解中国武术，让留学生在了解武术基本知识的同时感受武术对人民生活的影响，为他们进一步了解武术提供帮助，同时希望能够扩宽中高级水平汉语学生的文化视野，全面提升汉语水平。

　　希望您能喜欢《练武术》这本教材，也希望您对本书提出批评和建议。本书的编写得到了国家汉办的大力支持和帮助，在此一并表示感谢。

目录

第一课 【武术简介】
Lesson 1 【 Martial Arts - An Overview 】

① 野 兽　yěshòu
② 侵 略　qīnlüè
③ 兵 器　bīngqì
④ 拳 术　quánshù
⑤ 体 系　tǐxì
⑥ 防 御　fángyù
⑦ 陶 冶　táoyě

江一华：
今天看了《功夫熊猫》，真是太精彩了！

文小西：
我也很喜欢。这只熊猫又可爱又有正义感，里面的中国功夫也超级赞！

江一华：
就是！就是！本来我就对中国功夫很感兴趣，现在更着迷了。

文小西：
是吗？我对中国功夫完全不了解，你能给我介绍介绍吗？

江一华：
这……你可真难倒我了，我们还是问问大萌吧。

大 萌：
中国功夫，人们也称它为"中国武术"。你们猜猜，大概是什么时候开始出现武术的呢？

江一华:

　　大萌，你就别卖关子了，快告诉我们吧。

大　萌:

　　好吧。在原始社会，原始人类用木头和石头抵抗野兽或其他外敌的侵略，在这个过程中逐渐出现了原始的武术动作。

文小西:

　　现在算算，大概是五千年前了吧?

大　萌:

　　是的。后来社会不断发展，军队的建立与青铜器制造也促进了兵器的发展，中国武术逐渐成熟。

江一华:

　　什么时候形成了成熟、专门的武术呢?

大　萌:

　　根据不同资料记载，大约在唐代至明代时期形成了成熟的武术。武术可以分为武术基本理论、拳术、器械搏斗三部分。

文小西:

　　以前我以为武术只是打打架而已，没想到还有这么多学问。

大萌：

武术在历史发展中，逐渐发展成了与军事技术不同的一套体系，其健身价值也深受人们重视，到了清代，已发展成为一种"武术运动"。

江一华：

难怪每天早上我家楼下的花园里，有很多人一起练习武术呢，他们有的练太极拳，有的练剑术，有的练其他拳术。

大萌：

其实武术最重要的是传播一种精神，你们看看"武"这个字是由哪两个汉字组成的？

文小西：

我看到有"止"字，"停止"的"止"。

大萌：

没错。"武"是由"止"和"戈"两个字组成的。"止"就是停止，"戈"就是"武器"。所以"止""戈"就是停止使用武器，不要打仗的意思。

江一华：

也是对和谐、和平的向往吧。

大 萌：
　　是的。

中国武术历史悠久，影响深远。练习武术可以防御敌人、强身健体、陶冶性情和增进交流。武术常被分为"传统武术"与"现代武术"。传统武术重视攻防技术，而现代武术更重视健身和艺术表现，把"高、难、美、新"作为发展方向，现代武术还包括了 20 世纪 80 年代兴起的搏击运动。现代武术也是对传统武术的继承和发展，在沿袭传统武术部分实战模式的基础上，不断发展出竞技体育比赛和新竞技武术体系，形成了自己的特点。

①兴 起　xīngqǐ
②搏 击　bójī
③沿 袭　yánxí
④模 式　móshì
⑤实 战　shízhàn
⑥竞 技　jìngjì

Jiang Yihua: Today's *Kung Fu Panda* was such an exciting movie!

Wen Xiaoxi: I also enjoyed it a lot. That panda was cute and had a sense of justice. The kung fu shown was also totally amazing!

Jiang Yihua: I know, right? I was always interested in Chinese kung fu, but now I'm hooked.

Wen Xiaoxi: Really now? I don't know much about kung fu. Can you tell me more about it?

Jiang Yihua: About that… you've got me stumped. We better ask Da Meng.

Da Meng: Chinese kung fu, is also called "Chinese martial arts". Have a guess, about how many years ago do you think kung fu first made its appearance?

Jiang Yihua: Da Meng, don't keep us in suspense. Just tell us!

Da Meng: All right. In the earliest societies, people fought back wild beasts or invaders with wood and stones. It was during this time that the earliest martial moves gradually developed.

Wen Xiaoxi: Let's see… That should've been about 5,000 years ago?

Da Meng: Correct. Later, following continuous social development, the establishment of armies and manufacturing of bronze wares drove development of military weapons and Chinese martial arts matured.

Jiang Yihua: When did kung fu become mature and specialized?

Da Meng: According to different records, martial arts matured around the Tang to the Ming Dynasties. There are three components to kung fu: the basic theory, boxing and weapon fighting.

Wen Xiaoxi: I used to think that martial arts was just scuffling. I didn't think there was so much to it.

Da Meng: During their development in the past, martial arts gradually evolved into a system different from military technology. Their fitness value is also much appreciated by practitioners. They developed into "martial arts sports" by the Qing Dynasty.

Jiang Yihua: It's no surprise that there are many old people practicing martial arts together in the park downstairs every morning. Some practice Tai Chi, others sword fighting, and the rest (Chinese) boxing.

Da Meng: Martial arts are not only about health. Most importantly, they are about showing attitude. Look at the character of " 武 ". What radicals is it made up of?

Wen Xiaoxi: I'm seeing the " 止 " character, which means stop.

Da Meng: That's right. " 武 " is composed of the characters " 止 " and " 戈 ". " 止 " means "stop" and " 戈 " means "weapons". Therefore, together they mean "stop using weapons", or "stop making war".

Jiang Yihua: So martial arts are the strive for harmony and peace.

Da Meng: Correct!

Chinese martial arts have had a long history and far-reaching influence. Practicing martial arts can help in fighting off enemies, honing one's body, becoming even-tempered and building communication. Martial arts are often divided into "traditional martial arts" and "modern martial arts". Traditional martial arts prioritize offensive and defensive techniques, while modern martial arts attach more importance to fitness and artistic expression, with "style, difficulty, grace and novelty" dictating development trends. Modern martial arts also include combat sports, which rose in popularity in the 1980s. Modern martial arts continue the legacy and refinement of traditional martial arts. On the basis of continuing traditional martial arts'actual combat fighting methods, modern martial arts have given rise to new competitive sports tournaments and competitive martial arts systems and thus formed its own characteristics.

词 语

模 式
móshì
pattern; model; mode

侵 略
qīnlüè
commit aggression; invade

拳 术
quánshù
Chinese boxing

yě shòu 野 兽	wild beast; wild animal
bīng qì 兵 器	equipment
fáng yù 防 御	defend; guard
táo yě 陶 冶	cultivate; mould (one's temperament); nurture (character)
shí zhàn 实 战	actual combat; real combat

tǐ xì 体 系	system
xīng qǐ 兴 起	arise; rise
bó jī 搏 击	fight (as a sports category)
jìng jì 竞 技	athletic tournament
yán xí 沿 袭	continue (a tradition, pattern, etc.)

专有名词

清代 / Qīngdài / Qing Dynasty

语言点

1. 卖关子　　　　2. ……而……

思考

1. 请在表中填出不同时期武术的发展情况。

原始社会	
明代	
清代	

2. 你们国家有没有一种和武术相似的运动？请介绍一下。

3. 现代武术与传统武术相比有什么不同？

【武术的作用】
【The Role of Martial Arts】

> **江一华：**
> 大萌，我今天也起了个大早，在楼下跟着那些老人一起练习了剑术呢！

> **大萌：**
> 是吗？感觉怎么样？

> **江一华：**
> 真是太棒了，虽然我的动作不标准，也感觉不太适应，但练完以后，我出了一身汗，觉得身体轻松了不少。

> **大萌：**
> 看来你锻炼得不错嘛。俗话说："常常练武术，不用上药铺。""少时练得一身功，老来健壮不生病。"练习武术可以让人身心俱健。

> **文小西：**
> 一华，明天你去的时候也叫上我吧。我昨天在电视上看了一段太极拳表演，表演者是一位年轻的中国姑娘，她的动作缓慢中带着刚劲，柔软流畅，别提多美了，我一下子就迷上了！

大 萌：

这个提议不错，你俩一个练剑术，
一个练太极拳，说不定以后还可以
一起同台演出呢！

提到中国，许多外国人首先想到的可能就是武术。武术在竞技攻防、审美观赏、强身健体和教育交流等方面影响深远。在战争年代，攻防技击主要用于军事之中，是一个国家必备的军事技能之一。自古以来武术就有很强的艺术性和娱乐性，剑术表演、太极拳等都给人以审美享受。通过练拳习武，还可以对人进行武德教育，激发热情奋发的精神，武术界历来有"练拳兼修德"的格言。习武可以培养吃苦耐劳、坚持不懈的精神。练习基本功，可以磨炼"冬练三九，夏练三伏"的意志，"要练武，莫怕苦；要练功，莫放松。"由此可见，习武可以磨炼人的意志品质。

随着武术和武术文化的广泛传播，越来越多的人喜欢武术，练习武术，武友之间互相切磋，交流技艺，越来越多的武术爱好者也通过武术了解了中国文化。中国以"武"会友，与世界其他国家建立了友谊，增进了了解。

① 攻 防　　gōngfáng
② 观 赏　　guānshǎng
③ 技 击　　jìjī
④ 兼　　　jiān
⑤ 格 言　　géyán
⑥ 习 武　　xíwǔ
⑦ 吃苦耐劳　chīkǔ nàiláo
⑧ 坚持不懈　jiānchí búxiè
⑨ 切 磋　　qiēcuō
⑩ 莫　　　mò
⑪ 磨 炼　　móliàn
⑫ 以武会友　yǐwǔ huìyǒu
⑬ 增 进　　zēngjìn

Jiang Yihua: Da Meng, I also got up early in the morning today to practice sword fighting with the elderly downstairs!

Da Meng: Really now? What're your thoughts?

Jiang Yihua: Totally rad! My movements may have been not correct, and I was struggling to get the hang out of it all, but I sweated up a storm after my training and felt my entire body relaxing.

Da Meng: Sounds like you made the most of your training! As the saying goes, "Train hard when you're young and you'll be healthy and strong when you're old." Practicing martial arts can help both body and mind to be healthy.

Wen Xiaoxi: Yihua, when you're going tomorrow, give me a holler. I watched a tai chi performance on TV yesterday. The performer was a young Chinese girl. Her movements were slow, soft, fluid; simply beautiful. I immediately fell in love with it!

Da Meng: That's not a bad idea. One of you practices sword fighting, and the other tai chi. Maybe you can perform together on the same stage one day!

When mentioning China, it is martial arts that many people from other countries think of. Martial arts have deeply influenced offensive and defensive military combat, aesthetic standards, fitness training, education, communication and many other aspects. In the Warring States period, offensive and defensive martial arts techniques were mainly used in the military and were one of the necessary military skills a country had to have. Since ancient times, martial arts have had tremendous artistic and entertainment properties, with sword fighting performances and tai chi among many others having enjoyed much appreciation for their aesthetics. Practitioners of martial arts also receive education in martial arts virtues, develop passion and drive. Martial arts communities have always had the maxim of "training martial arts to cultivate virtues". Practitioners foster an indomitable spirit able to work hard and endure hardships. To temper your willpower, you can practice these fundamentals: train on the coldest and hottest days of the year; during training, do not be afraid and do not slack off. As you can see, practice of martial arts helps you sharpen your will. With the widespread dissemination of martial arts and its culture, more and more people enjoy martial arts, practice it, learn from each other and exchange skills. Increasingly more martial arts enthusiasts also get to know Chinese culture through martial arts. Through the exchange of martial arts, China and the world build friendship and promote understanding.

格言	géyán maxim; motto	**磨炼**	móliàn temper oneself; steel oneself; hone
切磋	qiēcuō learn from each otherby exchanging views		

jì jī 技 击	art of attack and defense in martial arts; fighting (methods)	gōng fáng 攻 防	attack and defend; offense and defense
xí wǔ 习 武	practice martial arts	jiān 兼	double; twice; simultaneous; combined
chī kǔ nài láo 吃 苦 耐 劳	work hard and endure hardships	jiān chí bú xiè 坚 持 不 懈	unremitting; persistent; keep going until the end
mò 莫	not; do not	guān shǎng 观 赏	look at sth. with pleasure; view and admire
yǐ wǔ huì yǒu 以 武 会 友	make friends through the exchange of martial arts	zēng jìn 增 进	enhance; further; advance; promote

专有名词

战国时期 / Zhànguó Shí qī / the Warring States Period

语言点

1. 对   2. 动词 + 于   3. 由此可见

思考

1. 根据课文，武术的作用是什么？

2. 你对"练武兼修德"怎么理解？

3. 你对课文中的武术谚语有什么看法？

第三课 Lesson 3

【武术文化】
【The Culture of Martial Arts】

大 萌:
　一华，你在看什么书呢？

江一华:
　我在看一本讲武术的书，书里介绍了武术的发展史，还讲了武术的作用。

大 萌:
　你真是个"武术迷"！

江一华:
　不过，书里常提到"武侠"这个词，这是什么意思呀？

大 萌:
　"武侠"是小说中的一类人物。侠，是"侠客""英雄"的意思。他们乐于帮助贫穷和弱小的人们，并且常常得到人们的认同和赞扬。

江一华:
　这样的英雄人物一定深受人们爱戴。

大 萌：

是的。这也是"武侠精神"，是古代练武人一生的追求，他们希望自己像英雄一样有高超的武功，也有英雄的高尚思想与品德。

江一华：

听你这么说，我也好想做一回"英雄侠客"！

大 萌：

俗话说，宝刀配英雄，在成为英雄侠客前你得有自己称手的兵器，你的兵器是什么啊？

江一华：

这个……我还真没有，我只练过"剑"，别的兵器都不太了解呢！

大 萌：

给你介绍两种古代常见的兵器：剑和棍。剑是金属做成的，非常锋利；棍是钝器，两种兵器的特征完全相反。

江一华：

我想，我还是比较喜欢剑，更锋利一些。

①武　侠	wǔxiá
②侠　客	xiákè
③涵　盖	hángài
④贫　穷	pínqióng
⑤高　超	gāochāo
⑥剑	jiàn
⑦棍	gùn
⑧钝　器	dùnqì
⑨门　派	ménpài
⑩怪　物	guàiwù
⑪制　服	zhìfú
⑫致　命	zhìmìng

　　武术和武术文化是中国传统文化的重要组成部分。武术与武侠精神、武术与兵器文化涵盖了中国哲学、传统医学等理论。武术文化提倡谦虚、以德会友、以和为贵，体现了中国传统文化"尊师重道""美善统一""清静无为"等思想。

　　古代练武之人对兵器都非常重视，兵器不但是练武和战斗的武器，也是一种精神的象征。中国武术门派当中的武当派信仰中国道教，他们常用剑，据说是因为道教认为剑能够消灭怪物；而少林派常用棍，他们信仰佛教，认为棍能够把对手制服，却不太会致命。

Da Meng: Jiang Yihua, what book are you reading?

Jiang Yihua: I'm reading a book about martial arts, which introduces the basic history and role of martial arts.

Da Meng: You're really a martial arts enthusiast!

Jiang Yihua: Anyway, the book often mentions "martial heroes". Who are those?

Da Meng: "Martial heroes" are characters in novels. Xia, derived from xia ke (follower of the xia), means "hero". They are ready to help the poor and weak, which earns them the approval and praise of these groups.

Jiang Yihua: Such heroes are certainly universally loved.

Da Meng: They are. This is also the spirit of martial arts chivalry, which martial arts practitioners were in pursuit of in ancient times. They hoped that they would be both superbly skilled in martial arts and have noble intentions as well as virtues just like heroes.

Jiang Yihua: Listening to your depiction, I also very much want to be a heroic follower of the xia!

Da Meng: As the saying goes, "A fine sword matches its hero". Before you become a heroic follower of the xia, you must have a fitting weapon of your own. What is yours?

Jiang Yihua: About that… I don't really have one. I only practiced the sword. I'm not familiar with any other weapons!

Da Meng: Then let me introduce you to two kinds of weapons commonly used in the olden days: the sword and the stick. Swords are made of metal and are very sharp, while sticks are blunt. Their characteristics are completely opposite of each other.

Jiang Yihua: I think I still prefer swords. I like their sharpness.

Martial arts and their culture are important components of traditional Chinese culture. Martial arts and the spirit of martial arts chivalry, martial arts and weapon culture cover the theories of Chinese philosophy and traditional medicine. Martial arts culture promotes modesty, friendship through virtues, harmony above all and as such embodies the traditional, cultural Chinese thinking such as "honoring the teacher and revering his teachings", "unity of beauty and benevolence" as well as the Daoist values of "tranquility" and "non-doing" .

Ancient practitioners of martial arts attached great importance to weapons. They served not only as weapons for martial arts and combat but were also a symbol of drive. The Chinese martial arts Wudang School believes in Chinese Daoism – they commonly use swords, allegedly because Daoists believe that swords can destroy monsters. The Shaolin School uses sticks because they believe in Buddhism and think that sticks are enough to subdue opponents, though they are less fatal.

词 语

怪 物	guàiwù
	monster

油	yóu
	oil; grease

wǔ xiá 武 侠	swordsman; martial arts chivalry; martial heroes
xiá kè 侠 客	martial artist following the code of xia; follower of xia; skillful martial artist given to chivalrous conduct
gāo chāo 高 超	superb; excellent
gùn 棍	stick
mén pài 门 派	school (group of followers of a particular doctrine)

hán gài 涵 盖	cover; contain; encompass
pín qióng 贫 穷	poor; impoverished
jiàn 剑	sword
dùn qì 钝 器	blunt instrument/ weapon
zhì mìng 致 命	cause death; fatal; deadly

专有名词

1. 佛教　　　/ Fó jiào / Buddhism
2. 道教　　　/ Dàojiào / Daoism (or Taoism)
3. 武当派　　/ Wǔdāng Pài / the Wudang School
4. 少林派　　/ Shǎolín Pài / the Shaolin School

语言点

1. 将　　　　　　2. 以和为贵

思考

1. 武侠和武侠精神是什么？

2. 为什么古代练武之人重视使用兵器？

3. 剑和棍各有什么特点？武当派和少林派分别用什么兵器？为什么？

第四课
Lesson 4

【武术派别】
【 Martial Arts Schools 】

（一）少林派

① 派别　pàibié
② 僧人　sēngrén
③ 风气　fēngqì

文小西：

大萌，我昨天看了《少林寺》那部电影，他们的功夫真是一流。你能给我具体讲讲少林寺的功夫吗？

大萌：

好，我先从中国武术的三大派别说起，首先是少林派。

江一华：

我听说过，就是少林寺的功夫。少林寺在河南，据说有不少武术迷专门跑去学功夫呢！

大萌：

在中国南北朝时期（420—589 年），为了强身健体，少林寺里的僧人形成了练武的风气。关于少林武术，有这样一个故事。

江一华：

说来听听。

大 萌：

传说在唐初，昙宗等十三位僧人帮助李世民作战，后来李世民当了皇帝，重重奖励了这十三个人。少林寺成了官方支持的练习武术的地方，少林寺逐渐兴旺，少林武术也开始繁荣。

文 小西：

《少林寺》这部电影讲的就是这个故事吗？

大 萌：

对，这部由李连杰主演的《少林寺》就来源于这段历史。在漫长的中华历史中，少林派不断改进，并在中国各地甚至全世界流传，成了中华武术之宗。

江 一华：

我看过一个节目，练武者表演的少林拳很像一些动物的动作，少林拳是不是在模仿动物动作的基础上改编而来的呢？

① 作 战 　zuòzhàn
② 兴 旺 　xīngwàng
③ 繁 荣 　fánróng
④ 武术之宗 　wǔshù zhīzōng

大 萌：

你说的是少林五拳，即龙拳、虎拳、豹拳、蛇拳和鹤拳，是从动物身上得到的灵感。"龙拳练神，虎拳练骨，豹拳练力，蛇拳练气，鹤拳练精。"

文 小西：

原来是这样，我去网上下载一个视频看看。

⑤豹　　　　bào
⑥门　派　　ménpài
⑦精　髓　　jīngsuǐ
⑧修　心　　xiūxīn
⑨禅武合一　chánwǔ héyī
⑩修　禅　　xiūchán
⑪套　路　　tàolù
⑫紧　凑　　jǐncòu
⑬敏　捷　　mǐnjié
⑭集大成者　jí dàchéngzhě

少林派是在河南少林寺拳术基础上形成的，是中国武术中范围最广、拳种最多的门派。少林武术的精髓就是倡导"习武"与"修心"相结合的"禅武合一"精神，练习这种武术的多为僧人，他们一边练武一边修禅，所以少林武术也叫"武术禅"。少林武术重视技击，突出"打"的功夫。它的所有动作套路完全从实战出发，严密紧凑，进退敏捷，以刚为主，以进攻为主，是各类外家拳法之集大成者。

（二）武当派

文小西：
　　大萌，太极拳属于哪个派别？

大萌：
　　这个问题目前还没有定论。部分学者认为太极拳属于武当派，是武当派武术中的一种拳。

①定　论　dìnglùn
②转　化　zhuǎnhuà
③御　敌　yùdí
④防　卫　fángwèi

林川：
　　武当派是谁创立的呢？

江一华：
　　是著名道士张三丰创立的吧。

王乐乐：
　　有这种说法，据说张三丰精通少林武术，但是他喜欢创新，把少林派的搏击进攻功夫转化成了御敌防卫的功夫，因为风格独特所以形成了新的武术派别——武当派。

江一华：
　　武当派和少林派的功夫有什么不同呢？

⑤以静制动　　yǐjìng zhìdòng
⑥以柔克刚　　yǐróu kègāng
⑦以弱胜强　　yǐruò shèngqiáng
⑧以慢胜快　　yǐmàn shèngkuài
⑨交　手　　　jiāoshǒu
⑩外柔内刚　　wàiróu nèigāng
⑪清静无为　　qīngjìng wúwéi
⑫养生之道　　yǎngshēng zhīdào
⑬圣　地　　　shèngdì
⑭约定俗成　　yuēdìng súchéng
⑮武术界　　　wǔshùjiè

王乐乐:

武当派更强调内功，以静制动，以柔克刚，以慢胜快，以弱胜强。简单地说，少林派强调进攻，武当派强调防守。

大萌:

是啊，虽然武当派太极拳的动作看起来缓慢温和，但交手时能感到强劲的力量，是一种外柔内刚的厉害功夫。

　　中国武术界中有"外家少林，内家武当"的说法，武当派也被叫作"内家拳"。武当派因湖北省武当山而得名。武当山是道教圣地，道教讲究清净无为，也讲究养生之道，所以武当拳的特点是技击与养生并重，将养生融于技击之中。目前，武术分类中已经不用"武当派"这一概念，只是大家约定俗成地把它看成是一种武术系类。

（三）峨眉派

大 萌：

今天我们来说说和四川佛教名山有关系的一个武术派别。

①猿 猴 yuánhóu
②创 编 chuàngbiān

江一华：

佛教名山？峨眉山？

大 萌：

对，这个武术派别叫峨眉派，是峨眉道人练习的武术。峨眉拳是在少林拳基础上，受猿猴技能特点启示，创编成的新拳术。

文小西：

是模仿峨眉山的猴子而编成的吗？

大 萌：

其实这些功夫并不是简单模仿，而是在对武术真正理解的基础上创作出来的。我们一起来看看这个拳术的表演吧。看，这个拳法最独特的就是伸臂和打击动作。

江一华：

我听说峨眉派还有兵器搏击术，是吧？

③潇 洒　xiāosǎ
④俊 美　jùnměi

大萌：

是的，有峨眉枪和峨眉剑。

江一华：

这两种有什么区别？

大萌：

峨眉枪用的是古代的一种"枪"，俗话说："枪为百兵之王，剑为百兵之秀。"枪在实战中威力强，剑练起来潇洒俊美。峨眉派的"峨眉枪""峨眉剑"的声誉都很高。

文小西：

枪和剑都太锋利了，有没有一些保持身材的功夫啊？

大萌：

有啊，你学"峨眉十二庄"吧。它最大的特点就是动静结合。与少林武术的"动"相比，"峨眉十二庄"更强调"静"，练习"峨眉十二庄"能强身健体，保持心情愉快，很适合女生呢。

文小西：

那我要学学！

　　峨眉武术发源于四川峨眉山，曾经是与少林、武当齐名的中华武术三大流派之一。峨眉派把健身、养生、文化融为一体，重视形体、呼吸的训练以及手法的运用和武术实用技术的练习，它的特点是动作时快时慢，刚柔结合，形式千变万化。

① 发 源　　fāyuán
② 齐 名　　qímíng
③ 融为一体　　róngwéiyītǐ

Part 1. The Shaolin School

Wen Xiaoxi: Da Meng, I watched a movie called *The Shaolin Temple* yesterday. Their kung fu really is top-notch! Can you tell us in detail what makes Shaolin kung fu special?

Da Meng: Sure. Let me tell you first about the three major schools of Chinese martial arts. Let's take about the Shaolin School first.

Jiang Yihua: I've heard that this is the kung fu practiced at Shaolin Temple, which is located in Henan. Allegedly, many martial arts enthusiasts specially go there to study kung fu!

Da Meng: During the Southern and Northern Dynasties (420-589), the Shaolin Temple monks established the practice of martial arts in order to keep fit. There's also this story about Shaolin martial arts.

Jiang Yihua: We're all ears!

Da Meng: Legend has it that at the beginning of the Tang Dynasty, thirteen monks including Tan Zong assisted Li Shimin in his war efforts. Later when Li Shimin became emperor, he rewarded these 13 people handsomely.

Shaolin Temple became an officially supported place for practicing martial arts, which helped the monastery to gradually thrive and made Shaolin martial arts begin to prosper.

Wen Xiaoxi: So does the plot of *The Shaolin Temple* tell this story?

Da Meng: Yes, *The Shaolin Temple* starred by Jet Li is based on this period. In China's long history, the Shaolin School continued to improve and spread throughout China and even the entire world, becoming the most prominent Chinese martial arts school.

Jiang Yihua: I watched a show where the martial artists performed Shaolin kung fu. Some movements looked just like those from animals. Are Shaolin kung fu moves based on and adapted from animal movements?

Da Meng: You're talking about the Shaolin Five Animal Fist style, namely Dragon Fist, Tiger Fist, Leopard Fist, Snake Fist and Crane Fist, which are inspired by animals. "Training the dragon cultivates your spirit; training the tiger strengthens your bones; training the leopard increases your power; training the snake cultivates your chi; training the crane promotes your vitality."

Wen Xiaoxi: So that's how it is! I'll go look for a video and download it.

The Shaolin School was formed based on the fighting techniques found in Shaolin Temple in Henan Province. It is the most common School with the most fists among Chinese martial arts. The essence of Shaolin martial arts is to promote the unity of mind and body by practicing kung fu and cultivating one's spirit. Most of the martial arts practitioners are monks who both practice kung fu and cultivate their spirits, which is why Shaolin martial arts is also called "zen martial arts". Shaolin martial arts focuses on fighting with special emphasis on strikes. All of its tight and nimble move sequences are completely based on actual combat and heavily favor strength and offence. It is the epitome of external martial arts.

Part 2. The Wudang School
(Scene: Da Meng, Wang Lele and several international students talk about martial arts in the café)

Wen Xiaoxi: Da Meng, what school does tai chi belong to?

Da Meng: The jury's still out. Some scholars believe that tai chi belongs to the Wudang School and is one of the styles they use.

Lin Chuan: Who founded the school?

Jiang Yihua: Was it the famous Daoist Zhang Sanfeng?

Wang Lele: Some say that Zhang Sanfeng was proficient in Shaolin martial arts. He liked innovating, though, so he transformed the offensive combat-focused Shaolin kung fu into a style of self-defense. By creating a unique style, he formed a new martial arts school: the Wudang School.

Jiang Yihua: What's difference between Wudang and Shaolin martial arts?

Wang Lele: The Wudang School emphasizes internal strength more. They believe in tranquility overcoming eagerness, softness besting hardness, in slowness trumping speed and achieving victory from a position of weakness. Put simply, Shaolin emphasizes offense, while Wudang prioritizes defense.

Da Meng: Right! Wudang's tai chi moves may appear slow and gentle, but their enemies may feel the sheer force behind these moves when trading blows. Their style appears to be yielding, but is firm in essence.

There is a saying in the world of Chinese martial arts: "Shaolin is the epitome of external martial arts, while Wudang is the embodiment of internal martial arts." Thus, the Wudang School is said to belong to the internal martial arts styles. The Wudang School is named after Wudang Mountain in Hubei Province. Mt. Wudang is sacred Daoist ground. Daoism is about tranquility, non-doing and maintaining good health. Therefore, Wudang boxing equally emphasizes combat and health. The way of maintaining health is an integral part of their offensive and defensive arts. The term "Wudang School" has not been officially used as a classification of martial arts – the name has been established by popular usage and stuck.

Part 3. The Emei School

Da Meng: Today we'll be talking about a martial arts school that shares ties with the famous Buddhist mountains in Sichuan.

Jiang Yihua: Buddhist mountains? Mt. Emei?

Da Meng: Correct! This martial art is called the Emei School and practiced by Emei Daoists. Their style is based on Shaolin arts, with inspirations taken from both apes and monkeys, and thus constitutes a new boxing art.

Wen Xiaoxi: Was it created based on the monkeys found on Mt. Emei?

Da Meng: We're not talking about a simple imitation. In fact, its creators had a deep understanding of martial arts. Let's look at this martial art show together. Did you see that? The way they extend their arms and attack is unique to this style.

Jiang Yihua: I heard that the Emei School also fights with weapons, right?

Da Meng: Right. They use their very own spears and swords.

Jiang Yihua: What's the difference between these two?

Da Meng: You might see the character (枪) and think it stands for "gun", but in ancient times, this character meant "spear". As the saying goes, "The spear rules the battlefield, while the sword entrances it." The spear possesses great power in actual combat, while the sword delivers a display of unrestrained beauty. The Emei School's spear and sword enjoy great prestige.

Wen Xiaoxi: Spears and swords are a bit too sharp for my taste. What about kung fu that keeps you fit?

Da Meng: They also have that! You can try to learn the "Emei Twelve Pillars" – their biggest feature is the combination of movement and stillness. Compared with Shaolin's "movement", the Twelve Pillars put more emphasis on "stillness". Practicing the Twelve Pillars can help you keep fit and maintain a good mood. It's perfect for girls!

Wen Xiaoxi: I'm sold!

The Emei style originated on Sichuan's Mt. Emei. It was once one of China's three major martial arts schools and equally famous with Shaolin and Wudang. The Emei School fuses fitness, health and culture into one, prioritizes physical and breathing training as well as use of techniques and practice of practical martial arts skills. The style is characterized by movement both fast and slow, and a unity of roughness and softness. Their combat form is ever-changing.

词语

修心

修	心	xiūxīn
		cultivate one's mind

强	劲	qiángjìn
		strong; powerful; forceful

pài bié 派 别	school
fán róng 繁 荣	flourishing; thriving; prosperous
bào 豹	leopard
jīng suǐ 精 髓	(quint-)essence
xiū chán 修 禅	cultivate one's spirit

zuò zhàn 作 战	fight; combat
wǔ shù zhī zōng 武 术 之 宗	the most prominent martial arts school
yǎng shēng 养 生	conserve one's vital powers; preserve one's health; keep in good health
chán wǔ hé yī 禅 武 合 一	unity of mind and body
tào lù 套 路	sequence of moves in martial arts

jǐn còu 紧 凑	compact
jí dà chéng zhě 集 大 成 者	synthesizer
zhuǎn huà 转 化	change; transform
fáng wèi 防 卫	defend
yǐ róu kè gāng 以 柔 克 刚	softness overcomes hardness
yǐ ruò shèng qiàng 以 弱 胜 强	using the weak to defeat the strong; to win from a position of weakness
wài róu nèi gāng 外 柔 内 刚	soft outside but hard inside; outwardly yielding but inwardly firm
yuē dìng sú chéng 约 定 俗 成	(of a name or social habit) established (or sanctioned) by popular usage; accepted through common practice; customary convention; everyone agrees that…

mǐn jié 敏 捷	agile
dìng lùn 定 论	conclude; reach a conclusion/ judgement
yù dí 御 敌	resist/ward off the enemy
yǐ jìng zhì dòng 以 静 制 动	tranquility overcomes eagerness
yǐ màn shèng kuài 以 慢 胜 快	slowness overcomes speed
shèng dì 圣 地	sacred place; holy land
qīng jìng wú wéi 清 静 无 为	tranquility and non- action/non-doing; the Daoist doctrines of calmness; an inaction
sēng rén 僧 人	(Buddhist) monk

wǔ shù jiè 武 术 界	the martial arts world; martial arts circles
xīng wàng 兴 旺	prosper; flourish; thrive
yuán hóu 猿 猴	apes and monkeys
xiāo sǎ 潇 洒	natural and unrestrained; confident and at ease; free and easy
fā yuán 发 源	rise; originate
róng wéi yī tǐ 融 为 一 体	fuse together

fēng qì 风 气	common/ established practice
jiāo shǒu 交 手	exchange of blows; fight hand to hand; be engaged in a hand-to-hand fight
chuàng biān 创 编	design; create
jùn měi 俊 美	pretty; handsome
qí míng 齐 名	enjoy equal popularity; be equally famous
qiáng jìn 强 劲	strong; powerful; forceful

专有名词

1. 少林寺 / Shǎolínsì / Shaolin Temple; Shaolin Monastery
2. 南北朝 / nánběicháo / the Northern and Southern Dynasties
3. 昙宗 / Tánzōng / Tan Zong
4. 李世民 / Lǐshìmín / Li Shimin
5. 张三丰（北宋著名道士） / Zhāngsānfēng / Zhang Sangfeng; (famous Northern Song Daoist)
6. 武当山 / Wǔdāngshān / Mt. Wudang
7. 峨眉山 / E méishān / Mt. Emei
8. 峨眉十二庄 / éméishíèrzhuāng / Emei Twelve Pillars

语言点

1. 从……出发……　2. A 与 B 相结合　3. 因……而……

4. 受……启示……　5. 与……齐名……

思考

1. 少林寺和少林派的关系是什么？

2. 除了"少林五拳"你还知道哪些少林派的功夫？

3. "武当派"和"少林派"各有什么特点？

4. "武当派"特点产生的原因是什么？

5. 这个部分介绍了"峨眉派"的哪些功夫？

6. 峨眉派的特点是什么？

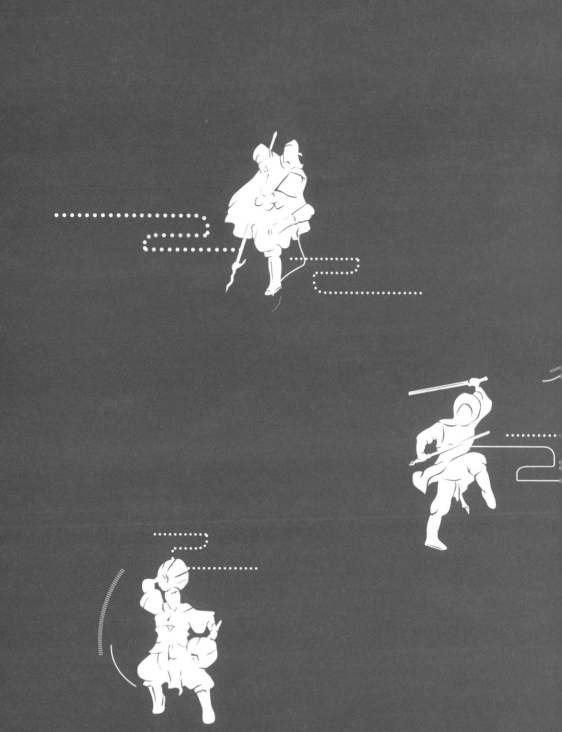

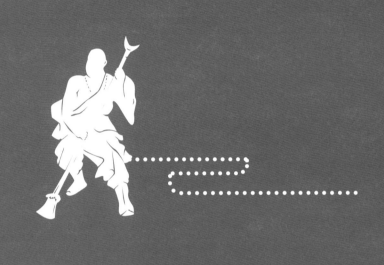

第五课 【留学生练武术】
Lesson 5 【International Students Practicing Martial Arts】

（情景：大萌和王乐乐来到留学生宿舍）

大萌：
林川，你收拾行李是要去旅游吗？

林川：
不是旅游，我和小西决定去峨眉山拜师学艺。

大萌：
你运气真好，世界传统武术锦标赛每两年举行一次，2017 年 11 月 7 日至 11 日这段时间正好在峨眉山举行第七届比赛。在这个比赛中你不仅可以看到各地武术高手，说不定还能拜个好师傅呢。

林川：
我们就是听说了这个消息，所以赶紧收拾行李出发，大萌，乐乐，你们给我们做导游吧。

大萌：
没问题，比赛结束之后我们带你们去参观一下峨眉山的中峰寺。

① 拜师学艺　bàishī xuéyì
② 战功赫赫　zhàngōng hèhè
③ 修　行　xiūxíng
④ 出　家　chūjiā
⑤ 记　载　jìzǎi
⑥ 拭目以待　shìmù yǐdài

文小西：

这个寺庙有什么特别的来历吗？

王乐乐：

在南朝的时候有位著名的和尚，叫"淡然大师"。他到峨眉山出家以前曾经是一位战功赫赫的将军。在中峰寺他一边修行，一边练武功，还把功夫教给僧人们，是峨眉山佛教史上有记载的第一位练习武术的僧人，为峨眉武术的发展打下了基础。

大萌：

是的。淡然大师还做过中峰寺的住持。

林川：

那我们得去参观参观，顺便感受一下宗教与武术之间的联系。

王乐乐：

不过，话说回来，学功夫可不容易，要做好吃苦的准备！

林川：

放心吧，有句话说："吃得苦中苦，方为人上人。"只要是我喜欢的，就不怕吃苦！

大萌：

加油，我们拭目以待！

(Scene: Da Meng and Wang Lele arrive at the international students' dormitory)

Da Meng: Lin Chuan, why are you packing your luggage? Are you going to travel?

Lin Chuan: No, Xiaoxi and I have decided to go to Mt. Emei and study under a master.

Da Meng: You're in luck! The World Traditional Wushu Championships are held once every two years. The seventh tournament is to be held on Mt. Emei from November 7 to November 11, 2017. There, you can not only see martial arts masters from every region, but maybe also take somebody talented as your teacher.

Lin Chuan: We've heard about this and this is exactly why we are in a hurry to pack our luggage and set off. Da Meng and Lele, could you guide us?

Da Meng: Sure. After the tournament is over, we'll take you to visit Zhongfeng Temple on Mt. Emei.

Wen Xiaoxi: Anything special about the origin of this temple?

Wang Lele: A famous monk called "The Indifferent Master" lived during the Southern Dynasty. Before he left his home to become a monk on Mt. Emei, he was a general with a track record of illustrious military exploits. He practiced both Buddhism and martial arts in Zhongfeng Temple and taught the monks kung fu. He was the first monk to practice martial arts in recorded history of Emei Buddhism and laid the foundation for developing Emei martial arts.

Da Meng: Correct. The Indifferent Master also served as the abbot at Zhongfeng Temple.

Lin Chuan: Then we have to go there for a visit and experience the bond between religion and martial arts for ourselves.

Wang Lele: But, again, studying kung fu is no easy task. You have to be prepared to endure hardship!

Lin Chuan: No worries. There is a saying, "Only if you can stand the hardest of hardships can you hope to become a better person." As long as I like what I do, I'm not afraid of enduring hardships!

Da Meng: Give it your all; we'll be waiting expectantly!

词语

战功赫赫	出家

战功赫赫 zhàngōng hèhè
illustrious military exploits; brilliant military success

出家 chūjiā
renounce the family (or to leave home) to become a monk or nun

bài shī xué yì 拜师学艺	learn a skill from a master; become an apprentice to a master in search of knowledge
xiū xíng 修行	practice Buddhism or Daoism

jì zǎi 记载	record; account
shì mù yǐ dài 拭目以待	wait and see; wait expectantly

语言点

为……打下基础

专有名词

1. 中峰寺　　　/ Zhōngfēng Sì / Zhongfeng Temple
2. 南朝　　　　/ Nán Cháo / Southern Dynasty
3. 淡然大师　　/ Dànrán Dàshī / The Indifferent Master

思考

> 1. 你去过峨眉山吗？在那儿你看到了什么？有什么体会？
>
> 2. 你如何理解和看待"吃得苦中苦，方为人上人"这句话？

第六课　【太极拳】
Lesson 6　【Tai Chi】

（一）太极拳简介

（林川、大萌、江一华、王乐乐在看新学期的课表）

① 天人合一　　tiānrén héyī
② 理　念　　　lǐniàn
③ 首　推　　　shǒutuī
④ 改　编　　　gǎibiān
⑤ 各有千秋　　gèyǒu qiānqiū
⑥ 纠　结　　　jiūjié

江一华：
我们学校还有太极拳的选修课，想得真周到。

林　川：
太极拳也是武术吗？

大　萌：
太极拳是中国传统武术项目之一，也是一种健身养生运动，是中国国家级非物质文化遗产，已经有几百年的历史了。

林　川：
武术、健身、养生，听起来不错。

王乐乐：
太极拳是一种阴柔的拳，以中国传统哲学的"太极""阴阳""天人合一"核心理念为基础，结合古代阴阳五行学说、中医经络学、古代气功和呼吸养生功法创立的拳种，有防身技击、强身健体、静心养生、修炼自我的作用。

江一华：

太极拳应该也有很多种类吧？如果我想学太极拳的话，学哪种好呢？

王乐乐：

太极拳包括传统太极拳和现代太极拳。传统太极拳由传人代代相传至今，著名的太极拳流派有陈式、杨式、武式、吴式等。现代太极拳是对传统太极拳的部分动作和招式进行简化而来的。

大萌：

比较流行的现代太极拳首推在中国家喻户晓的"24式简化太极拳"。它有24个动作招式，是根据杨式太极拳改编的，在中国大部分中学和大学里的体育课都会教。

大萌：

除此之外还有"48式简化太极拳"，是综合陈式、杨式、武式、孙式和吴式等著名流派的优点改编而成的，有48个动作招式，打起来也挺漂亮的。

王乐乐：

我认为如果想系统学习太极拳功夫、深入体会太极拳文化的话，还是学传统太极拳吧。

⑦见 识　　jiànshi
⑧一言为定　yīyán wéidìng

江一华:

为什么，有什么讲究吗？

王乐乐:

我个人觉得简化太极拳套路确实好学，不过招式动作太少，运动量不够，也很难进入到全身经络通顺的太极拳状态。

大萌:

乐乐说得挺在理的。如果从强身健体和养生的效果来说，学传统太极拳当然更理想。

林川:

实话说，我对现代太极拳和传统太极拳都有兴趣，因为两者各有千秋。先学哪种拳，我真是好纠结啊！

王乐乐:

这样吧，这个周末我和大萌带你们去人民公园见识见识。那儿有很多人练不同的太极拳。你们可以先体会一下。

江一华:

太好了！一言为定！

⑨刚柔并济　gāngróu bìngjì
⑩防　身　fángshēn
⑪自　卫　zìwèi
⑫修　炼　xiūliàn
⑬招　式　zhāoshì
⑭人　士　rénshì

太极拳包括传统太极拳和现代太极拳。传统太极拳大约在 19 世纪中期形成，是一种以防御为主、以柔克刚、节奏均匀缓慢的拳术，讲究刚柔并济，重视身体和精神共同修炼。传统太极拳除了各流派单独的拳技套路以外，还包括太极推手、太极大杆、太极枪等功夫的练法。现代太极拳是近现代特别是从 1949 年建立新中国以来在传统太极拳的基础上进行改革后形成的一些太极拳，主要包括中国国家体育部门组织改编的各种太极拳套路，比如太极拳普及推广套路、竞赛套路，还有民间武术人士创编的一些太极拳新套路等。现代太极拳简化了传统太极拳的部分动作和招式，弱化了太极拳技击对抗和防身自卫的功能，保留了其强身健体和运动养生的功能，对推动全民健身起到了重要作用。

（二）太极拳的基础理论与养生作用

①万 物　wànwù
②意 念　yìniàn

> **文**小西：
> 　　请问，太极拳的"太极"是什么意思啊？

> **王**乐乐：
> 　　"太极"就是"阴"和"阳"混合的状态，是宇宙最开始的静止状态。

> **文**小西：
> 　　阴和阳，不太懂呢。

> **大**萌：
> 　　中国古人认为世界万物都由阴阳两部分组成。比如，黑夜和白天是阴和阳；地和天、水和火也是阴和阳。

> **马**兰：
> 　　所以阴和阳就是矛盾对立的两部分吗？

> **大**萌：
> 　　是的。随着太极的运动，阴阳逐渐分化对立，并且相互转化，和谐发展，最后产生出宇宙万物。

王乐乐：

　　太极拳就是用太极阴阳的道理来概括和解释拳法的各种变化，比如，太极的刚柔关系里，"刚"代表阳，"柔"代表阴。太极拳在运动中强调身体各部位相互协调，从而达到身体与精神的高度和谐，这就是"天人合一"。

马 兰：

　　太极拳是怎么让练习者达到身体与精神和谐的目的？

王乐乐：

　　首先，太极拳要求练习者内心安静，身体放松，集中意念，所谓"身随心动"就是用意念引导动作进行运动。让身体与精神高度协调。

马 兰：

　　练习太极拳是怎么起到养生健身的作用的呢？

大萌:

太极拳是基于中医经络学理论创编的，在运动中每个招式动作要求符合人体骨骼的最佳受力状态，运动路线走弧形、圆形，达到人体气血和经络通畅，并在运动中配合深沉均匀的呼吸，这对人体新陈代谢、血液循环等都十分有利。另外，太极拳强调用意念引导动作，这既可帮助练习者增强身体灵敏性，又可避免运动中身体部位的损伤，同时还可帮助练习者改变自身一些不当的用力和呼吸习惯，提高身体的自我控制力与保护力。

③损 伤　sǔnshāng
④不 当　búdàng
⑤融 入　róngrù
⑥偏 激　piānjí
⑦融 合　rónghé
⑧采 用　cǎiyòng
⑨大有裨益　dàyǒu bìyì

王乐乐:

不仅如此，练太极还有利于人们提高自我修养。可以这么说，练习太极拳的最高境界是通过修炼身体达到修炼心性，并且把太极理论融入生活和工作中去，做人做事有分寸，不偏激。因此，可以说练太极是一种寻找身心融合、和谐发展的自我再造过程。

　　太极拳跟中国其他传统武术一样，深受中国古典传统文化的影响，特别受道家文化的影响。太极拳采用了道教传统的气功和呼吸术，同时又结合古代中医经络学说，形成了练意识、练呼吸、练内气、练身形等内外统一的特点，对养生健身有积极作用。另外，太极拳拳架可高可低，运动量可大可小，室内室外均可，练拳者可根据个人情况来选择。总之，太极拳是一种全身各部位共同参与锻炼的有氧运动，对于健康大有裨益，适合不同年龄和体质的人练习。

目前，太极拳已经在 150 多个国家和地区传播，全世界练习者人数超过 3 亿。太极拳是十分理想的绿色保健养生运动。

（三）太极拳的技击作用和特点

①趁其不备　chènqí bùbèi
②挫 败　　　cuòbài

马 兰：

我有一个疑惑，想请教一下你们。我看太极拳动作那么缓慢柔和，会有技击的作用吗？

大 萌：

太极拳是武术，当然有技击的作用，只是如果不懂得正确的练法就体会不到它的真功夫。

王 乐乐：

对。太极拳是外柔内刚的拳术，要求用意不用力，真正的太极拳动作外表看上去很柔和，其实里面充满了劲力。

江 一华：

我爷爷曾经告诉我太极拳功夫很厉害，他说太极拳不主动进攻对手，而是以防为攻，在跟对手交手中先顺着对方，然后找到对方力量弱点，趁其不备，破坏对手的平衡，利用反作用力让对手挫败。

大 萌：

对！这就是太极拳的借力打力。

王 乐乐：

是的。以静制动、以慢胜快、借力打力、以弱胜强等特点是太极拳在技击战术上的独到之处。

林 川：

为什么太极拳不讲究主动出击呢？

王 乐乐：

这是因为太极拳在技击战术上吸收了道家顺其自然、无为而为、以柔克刚的思想，在技击时，讲求不争先，不主动出击，而是根据对方的动作变化来确定灵活的战术。

江 一华：

所以太极拳功夫也有技击的作用。

王 乐乐：

没错。作为武术的太极功夫最开始就是用来抗击打、保平安的。

马 兰：

听起来好酷！我忍不住想学几招太极拳功夫了。

大萌:

好呀，如果你会太极功夫，你的自我防卫能力就会大大提升的。

王乐乐:

太极拳有一个基本功——太极推手。在传统太极拳的教学中，师傅会把太极拳套路中的招式拆开给徒弟看，手把手地跟徒弟一起演示每个招式，告诉学生每一个招式的攻防含义。

大萌:

这就是"拆拳""拆招儿"。这样，学生才能明白太极拳的拳理和拳法。

林川:

哦。原来是这样的。对了，太极拳有那么多流派。它们之间有没有什么共同点呢？

王乐乐:

有呀。比如在身体姿势方面都要求立身正中，头顶往上悬，沉肩垂肘，含胸拔背等，在运动路线上都要求弧形运转等。动作速度要以柔和缓慢为主，全身放松等其他很多要求。

林 川:

你们这么一说，我对学太极拳的兴趣越来越大了。

⑫纪录片　　jìlùpiān
⑬格斗术　　gédòushù

马 兰:

我也是。

大 萌:

太极拳只有通过练习才能慢慢感受它究竟是怎么一回事。

王 乐乐:

对了，我推荐你们上网看一看纪录片《最高境界的格斗术》。这是陈式太极拳第11代传人张志俊代表中国太极拳第一次走进国家体育科学实验室，对太极拳"以柔克刚"、以小力胜大力的特点进行科学测试，用科学数据说明太极拳的特点。

林 川、江一华:

太好了！我今晚就看。

（四）太极拳三大流派

（江一华、文小西、林川、马兰、大萌、王乐乐在茶馆里聊天）

① 发源地　fāyuándì
② 创始人　chuàngshǐrén
③ 家　传　jiāchuān

王乐乐：

我考考你们，中国传统太极拳有哪三个最著名的流派？

江一华：

这个难不倒我。这三个流派分别是陈式太极拳、杨式太极拳、武式太极拳。

王乐乐：

答对了，厉害！从时间上看，陈式太极拳最早创立。其他太极拳是在它的基础上发展演变来的。不过也有些研究太极拳的人认为这个说法不太准确。

林川：

陈式太极拳，我猜它的创始人姓陈吧？

王乐乐：

没错。陈式太极拳陈拳的发源地在河南，创始人叫陈王廷。他在家传武功基础上，学习和吸收了当时流行的主要拳法，融合了一些古代道家养生修炼功法，同时结合古代太极阴阳理论和中医经络学说，创编出了一套太极拳的练习方法。这套拳既能防身抗暴，又能强身健体。后来人们把这个拳法叫作"陈式太极拳"。

江一华：

听说当初陈氏家族专门规定功夫不外传。

王乐乐：

是的，而且还规定只有本家族里的男人才能练习和传承此拳。

林川：

真的吗？那后来是什么原因让陈拳走出了陈家呢？

江一华：

是这样的。陈拳的第 14 代传人陈长兴对这个家传功夫进行了改进，并且打破家规，开设武馆对外教拳，于是陈拳得到了传播。

王乐乐：

对！当年有一个跟陈长兴学拳的外族人叫杨露禅，他学到功夫后就根据自己学拳、练拳和教拳的经验，对陈拳进行简化，简化后的招式更容易施展，动作更柔和顺畅，内在功夫也在不知不觉中得到了练习。这种更适合普通人练习的太极拳习练方法被人们称为"杨式太极拳"。杨拳出现后，练习太极拳的人越来越多，太极拳随之传遍大江南北。

④ 传承　chuánchéng
⑤ 打破　dǎpò
⑥ 开设　kāishè
⑦ 武馆　wǔguǎn
⑧ 外族　wàizú
⑨ 施展　shīzhǎn
⑩ 顺畅　shùnchàng
⑪ 大江南北　dàjiāng nánběi
⑫ 功不可没　gōngbù kěmò
⑬ 舒展　shūzhǎn

林 川：

这么说太极拳在中国普及，杨露禅功不可没！

王 乐乐：

说得对！

文 小西：

那么陈拳和杨拳各有什么主要特点呢？

王 乐乐：

简单说，陈拳比较注重技击性，讲究爆发力，比其他太极拳更能表现武术的技击功夫。从动作外形上看，刚柔结合，快慢相间，速度变化比较明显。陈拳跳跃动作比较多，动作难度比较高。

文 小西：

哦。可以想象陈拳打起来一定很帅。那杨拳呢？

王 乐乐：

杨拳的动作看起来舒展大方，打拳的速度比较缓慢均匀，动作难度比较低，容易掌握，而且养生健身的功能更强，所以深受普通老百姓喜爱，可以说对男女老少都适合。

文 小西：

哦，怪不得一个中国朋友告诉我他身边会杨拳的人比会陈拳的人多。

⑭ 坚实　jiānshí
⑮ 褂　　guà
⑯ 含蓄　hánxù
⑰ 简洁　jiǎnjié

林 川：

乐乐，我听说武拳是"书生拳"？这是怎么回事呢？

王 乐乐：

书生在中国古时候是读书人的意思。武拳之所以被叫作"书生拳"，是因为它是由清代道光年间一个叫武禹襄的读书人在陈式太极拳和赵堡太极拳的基础上编创出来的，并且是在文化人中传承和习练。另外，武拳很重视太极拳理论研究，拳法有坚实的理论基础。

林 川：

那武拳有什么主要特点呢？

王 乐乐：

武拳是文人创立的拳，也是文人练的拳。过去的文人穿长袍大褂，走路动作幅度小，不迈大步，同时文人特别讲究文雅含蓄，所以练功的时候武拳的拳架子比较高，动作姿势比较紧凑，步法灵活多变，整个拳的动作转换和节奏十分清晰。另外，武拳特别重视内在功夫，要求外形招式简洁。

马兰:

哦，我明白了。

王乐乐:

你们如果对太极拳感兴趣的话，不妨多了解一下太极拳理论，读一读王宗岳的《太极拳论》吧。这是太极拳理论最重要的书。

林川:

好的。我记下来了。对了，武式和杨式太极拳的发源地也是河南吗？

王乐乐:

不是，这两个拳的发源地都是在河北省永年县，杨露禅和武禹襄都是永年人。

林川:

哦。那在成都有没有厉害的传统太极拳传人呢？

王 乐乐：

　　成都的传统太极拳师傅可不少呢。比如杨式太极拳第 5 代传人陈龙骧。

林 川：

　　太好了。我要学太极拳。你哪天给我介绍一位老师吧。

文 小西、马兰：

　　我们也想学。

王 乐乐：

　　没问题。

　　关于太极拳的起源和创始人，历史上有几种不同的说法。民间传说中，著名道士张三丰通常被认为是太极拳的始祖。根据一些武术史学家考证，河南温县陈家沟是太极拳发源地，现在传播的各式太极拳都是从陈家沟陈氏族人传习的拳法发展而来的，明末清初拳师陈王廷是此拳法的创始人。从中国武术的发展历史来看，太极拳综合吸收了许多朝代尤其是明代武术名家的枪法、剑术和各种拳法的优点而创立出来的独特拳种。明代的王宗岳、蒋发，清代的陈长兴、陈清平、杨露禅和武禹襄等著名武术家和拳师在太极拳理论、方法、发展和普及上做出了重大贡献。

Part 1 Tai chi – An Overview

(Lin Chuan, Da Meng and Jiang Yihua are looking at the schedule of electives for the new semester)

Jiang Yihua: Our school offers a tai chi elective. How considerate of them!

Lin Chuan: Is tai chi also a martial art?

Da Meng: Tai chi is one of China's traditional martial arts disciplines. It is a sport that promotes both fitness and health. It belongs to China's national intangible cultural heritage and has a history of several hundred years.

Lin Chuan: Martial arts, fitness, health – all in one package!

Wang Lele: Tai chi is a martial art with round and soft movements, based on the core concepts found in traditional Chinese philosophy: the "Supreme Ultimate", "yin and yang", and "heaven and humanity are one". This style combines the ancient Chinese theories of yin-yang and the five elements, TCM's meridian system, qigong, breathing training and health conservation. It is about self-defense, physical fitness, meditation and self-cultivation.

Jiang Yihua: Tai chi probably comes in many styles, right? If we want to study tai chi, which should I go for?

Wang Lele: Tai chi includes traditional and modern forms. The traditional form has been handed down from generation to generation, with the famous tai chi schools being Chen, Yang, Wu (Hao) and Wu. Modern tai chi is a simplification of some of the actions and moves of traditional tai chi.

Da Meng: There's also the "Simplified Tai chi 48 Postures", which is a compilation of the best various styles have to offer. It boasts 48 moves and looks gorgeous in execution.

Lin Chuan: Sounds great! Do you guys think I should learn modern or traditional?

Ma Lan: But why? Is there anything particular about traditional tai chi?

Wang Lele: I personally feel that while the simplified tai chi forms may be easy to learn, they lack in moves and you don't get a lot physical exercise out of them. It is difficult to get into the state of taiji quan, where energy flows smoothly within the meridians of the whole body.

Da Meng: Lele raises a good point. For improving fitness and health, studying traditional tai chi is certainly a better idea.

Ma Lan: I've really learnt a lot today. Thank you, Lele and Da Meng, for your explanations and suggestions!

Lin Chua: To be honest, I'm actually interested in both modern and traditional tai chi because they both have their merits. Which to learn first? I'm at a loss!

Wang Lele: Let's do it like this: Da Meng and I will take you to the People's Park this weekend, so you can learn more. There are many people there who practice different styles of tai chi. You can see for yourselves what style you prefer.

Lin Chuan, Wen Xiaoxi and Ma Lan: Great! It's settled then!

Wang Lele: I think if you want to learn tai chi systemically and acquire a deep understanding of its culture, you should go for traditional tai chi.

Tai chi comes in traditional and modern training forms. Traditional tai chi was formed around the mid-19th century. It is a boxing technique focusing on defense, softness and an even, slow rhythm. It couples strength and gentleness and equally emphasizes practice of both body and spirit. In addition to the separate boxing moves of the various schools, traditional tai chi also includes training in tai chi pushing hands, tai chi long pole and tai chi spear. Modern tai chi is a contemporary, revamped form of traditional tai chi, which especially began to spread since the People's Republic of China's establishment in 1949. It mainly includes various tai chi forms compiled by the Chinese Sports Commission, which include popular and competitive forms as well as those created by non-governmental martial arts practitioners. Modern tai chi simplifies some of the actions and moves of traditional tai chi, cuts back on the counterattack and self-defense aspects, but retains its fitness and health benefits, playing an important role in promoting national fitness.

Part 2   Tai Chi's Theoretical Foundation and Its Role in Health Preservation

(Wen Xiaoxi, Wang Lele, Da Meng and Ma Lan discuss tai chi)

Wen Xiaoxi: May I ask what the "taiji" in tai chi means?

Wang Lele: "Taiji" is the mixed state of "Yin and Yang" and was the resting state of the universe at the start.

Wen Xiaoxi: "Yin" and "Yang", I don't get it.

Da Meng: The ancient Chinese believed that everything in the world is composed of two parts: yin and yang. Night and day are yin and yang respectively; the earth and the sky, water and fire are also yin and yang.

Ma Lan: So, yin and yang are two contradictory parts?

Da Meng: They are. With the movement of the taiji, the yin and yang gradually divided and opposed each other, but also transformed each other, developed harmoniously and finally produced everything in the universe.

Wang Lele: Tai chi uses the concepts of taiji, yin and yang to generalize and explain various changes in fighting techniques. Let's take a look at the principles of "hardness" and "softness" in tai chi. "Hardness" represents yang, while "softness" stands for yin. It stresses the coordination of various parts of the body in order to achieve a high degree of harmony between body and spirit. This is "heaven and man are one".

Ma Lan: How does tai chi enable its practitioners to achieve harmony between body and spirit?

Wang Lele: First, tai chi requires the practitioner to be quiet inside, physically relax and concentrate their thoughts. What is known as"mind over matter" refers to using one's will to guide one's movements, making your body and your mind act in concert.

Ma Lan: And how does practicing tai chi help with keeping fit and healthy?

Da Meng: Tai Chi's moves are created on the basis of TCM's meridian theory. Every move and action has to be in accordance with the best skeletal alignment. During exercise, one moves in arcs and curves, enabling qi and blood to circulate freely. Movement is paired with deep, uniform breathing, which is of great benefit to the metabolism, blood circulation and so on. What's more, tai chi's focus on using will to guide movement not only helps the practitioner to make their body more agile but also help avoid injury when exercising. It also helps the practitioner to change some of their bad exertion and breathing habits and improves the body's self-control and protective abilities.

Wang Lele: It's not only that, practice of tai chi is beneficial for cultivating oneself. The highest level of practicing tai chi is about cultivating one's nature through cultivating one's body and integrating tai chi theory into everyday life and work. It means that, whoever you are and whatever you do, you know your limits and don't go to extremes. Therefore, it can be said that practicing tai chi is a process of harmonious self-reconstruction, where the practitioner seeks physical and mental unity.

Tai chi, like other traditional Chinese martial arts, is deeply influenced by classical traditional Chinese culture, particularly by Daoist culture. Tai chi uses traditional Daoist qi gong and breathing techniques, which it combines with the ancient meridian theory of traditional Chinese medicine at the same time to improve awareness, breathing, internal energy, and one's figure. As such, it has a positive effect on health and fitness. Furthermore, in tai chi, your stance may be high or low, the amount of exercise can be large or small, you can practice indoors or outdoors – the practitioner may train to their own liking. In short, tai chi is an aerobic exercise, which exerts all parts of the body. It provides great health benefits and is suitable for people of all ages and constitutions.

Tai chi has spread to more than 150 countries and regions, with the global number of practitioners exceeding 300 million. Tai chi is an ideal environmentally friendly health exercise.

Part 3 Fighting Methods of Tai Chi

(Ma Lan, Jiang Yihua, Da Meng, Wang Lele and Lin Chuan are talking about tai chi)

Ma Lan: There's something I don't get, and I'd like to ask you guys. Tai chi movements are so slow and gentle; is it really fit for fighting?

Da Meng: Tai chi is a martial art, so of course it is. Only if you not practice correctly would you not experience its kung fu.

Wang Lele: Correct. Tai chi is a style that is outwardly yielding but inwardly firm and requires its practitioner to rely on their will instead of brute force. Genuine tai chi moves may appear gentle, but, in fact, they burst with inherent strength.

Jiang Yihua: My grandpa once told me that tai chi kung fu packs quite a punch. He said that tai chi isn't about taking the initiative to attack, and it's about self-defense. You first move with the enemy attacks and then find an opening, catch them off guard, disrupt their balance, redirect their attack and thus defeat the opponent.

Da Meng: Right! Tai chi is about using the enemy's strength against them.

Wang Lele: It is. This is what sets tai chi apart from other martial arts: calm and slow movements focused on counterattacking that help its practitioner defeat a superior opponent.

Lin Chuan: Why doesn't tai chi prioritize taking the initiative?

Wang Lele: This is because tai chi has assimilated the Daoist teachings of "letting nature take its course", "doing by non-doing" and "overcoming hardness with softness". In a fight, tai chi doesn't emphasize being the first to strike and taking the initiative; decisions are made on the fly according to the opponent's movements.

Jiang Yihua: So tai chi can indeed be used for fighting.

Wang Lele: That's right. Tai chi as a martial art was at first practiced to fight back and protect peace.

Ma Lan: That sounds so cool! I can't help but wanting to learn a few tai chi moves myself.

Da Meng: Sure! If you know tai chi, your capabilities of self-defense will greatly increase.

Wang Lele: There's a basic skill in tai chi called "pushing hands". When teaching traditional tai chi, the master breaks down individual moves within sequences to show them to their apprentices. The master gives instructions as they demonstrate every single move to the apprentices and explains the offensive and defensive purposes.

Da Meng: This is called "breaking down the strikes" and "breaking down the moves". Only in this way are the apprentices able to grasp the inner workings and the techniques of tai chi.

Lin Chuan: Oh. So that's how it is. By the way, there are so many tai chi schools. Do they share anything in common?

Wang Lele: They sure do! In terms of body posture, for example, they all require a standing centered body, the head lifted upright, sunken shoulders and dropped elbows, sunken chest and raised back and so on. They also require movements to curve, and much more. The pace should be primarily soft and slow, and the whole body relaxed. These are only are a few of many more requirements.

Lin Chuan: Listening to you has made me more and more interested in learning tai chi.

Ma Lan: Me too.

Da Meng: Only through training can you gradually experience for yourself what tai chi is all about.

Wang Lele: By the way, I recommend watching the documentary *The Highest Level of Martial Arts*. It shows Zhang Zhijun, who is the 11th generation successor of Chen-style tai chi and a representative of Chinese tai chi, as he enters a laboratory of the China Institute for Sports Science and conducts scientific tests on tai chi's characteristics of "softness overcoming hardness" and "the small conquering the big". He uses science to show the features of tai chi.

Lin Chuan and Jiang Yihua: Awesome! I'll go watch it tonight.

Part 4   The Three Big Schools of Tai Chi

(Jiang Yihua, Wen Xiaoxi, Lin Chuan, Ma Lan, Da Meng and Wang Lele chat in a teahouse)

Wang Lele: I'll quiz you – what are the three most famous schools of Chinese traditional tai chi?

Jiang Yihua: No problem! The three schools are Chen-style, Yang-style and Wu-style tai chi.

Wang Lele: You're correct! Terrific! Chronologically speaking, Chen style was founded first. The other styles developed on its basis. Having said that, some scholars of tai chi think that this statement isn't accurate.

Lin Chuan: Talking about Chen-style tai chi, I guess its founder's last name was Chen?

Wang Lele: You're right. The birthplace of Chen-style tai chi is Henan and its founder was Chen Wangting. With the kung fu handed down in his family as the foundation, he studied and absorbed the main boxing methods that were popular at that time, integrated some ancient Daoist health cultivation exercises and combined the ancient taiji yin-yang principle and TCM's meridian theory into a set of tai chi practice methods. This style is not only useful for warding off aggressors, it also keeps fit. Later on, this style was called "Chen-style tai chi".

Jiang Yihua: I heard that the Chen clan initially ruled their kung fu not to be taught to outsiders.

Wang Lele: True. They also ruled that only the men in their family may practice and pass on their kung fu.

Lin Chuan: Really? Then how come Chen-style tai chi spread outside the clan?

Wang Lele: It went like this: Chen Changxing, the 14th generation descendant, improved the family's martial arts. He broke the rules of the family and opened a martial arts center to teach his kung fu to outsiders. Consequently, Chen-style kung fu spread.

Wen Xiaoxi: Chen Changxing was open-minded!

Wang Lele: He sure was! An outsider called Yang Luchan studied kung fu with Chen Changxing in the same year. After learning, he simplified Chen-style tai chi based on his studying, practicing and teaching experience. The simplified style was easier to perform, the movements were softer and smoother, and the internal kung fu could also be practiced unconsciously. This type of tai chi practice that is more suitable for common people is known as"Yang-style tai chi". After this style made its debut, tai chi was practiced by more and more people and spread all over the country.

Lin Chuan: Putting it like that, tai chi's popularity has been in no small part thanks to Yang Luchan!

Wang Lele: Right!

Wen Xiaoxi: So what are the main characteristics of Chen-style and Yang-style tai chi?

Wang Lele: Simply put, Chen-style focuses on attack and explosive force and lets its practitioner be more effective in fighting compared to other forms of tai chi. Talking about its movements, they are a combination of rough and soft, an alternation of fast and slow and the change in speed is more obvious. There are more jumps and the movements are more difficult to pull off.

Wen Xiaoxi: Oh. I can just imagine how cool Chen-style must look. What about Yang style?

Wang Lele: Its movements appear to stretch gracefully, its speed of striking is relatively slow and uniform, the difficulty of its movements is relatively low, it is easier to master, and is health and fitness benefits are more pronounced. Therefore, it is loved by ordinary people and can be said to be suitable for people of all ages.

Wen Xiaoxi: Oh, no wonder a Chinese friend told me that he knows more people who practice Yang style than Chen style.

Lin Chuan: Lele, I heard that the Wu form is the"Form for Students of the Book". What's that supposed to mean?

Wang Lele: In ancient China, "students of the book"meant"scholar". The reason why Wu form was called "Form for the Students of the Book" or the"Scholar's Form" is that it was compiled on the basis of Chen-style and Zhao Bao-style by a scholar named Wu Yuxiang during Daoguang's reign in the Qing Dynasty. It was a style passed on and studied among intellectuals. In addition, this style focuses on the study of tai chi theory and its fighting technique has a solid theoretical basis.

Lin Chuan: What are the main traits of Wu form?

Wang Lele: Wu form was created and practiced by intellectuals. In the past, intellectuals wore large robes and walked in small steps; they didn't make big strides. They were refined and reserved, so, during practice, their stance was relatively high, their movements and postures relatively compact and their footwork flexible and varied. Shifting between movements and changing the rhythm were incredibly clear. In addition, Wu form attaches special importance to internal kung fu and requires the outer moves to be simple.

Ma Lan: Oh, I get it!

Wang Lele: If you're interested in tai chi, you might want to learn more about tai chi theory and Wang Zongyue's *Tai Chi Treatise*. It is the most important book on tai chi theory.

Lin Chuan: Okay, noted. By the way, is the birthplace of Wu style and Yang style also Henan?

Wang Lele: No, that would be Yongnian County in Hebei Province. Yang Luchan and Wu Yuxiang come from Yongnian.

Lin Chuan: Oh. So are there any skillful disciples of traditional tai chi in Chengdu?

Wang Lele: There are quite a lot, actually, for example Chen Longfu, the fifth generation successor of Yang style.

Lin Chuan: Great! I want to learn tai chi. Please introduce me a teacher someday.

Wang Lele: Sure thing.

There are many different theories about the origin and founder of tai chi. In folklore, famous Daoist Zhang Sanfeng is often considered the ancestor of tai chi. According to the research of some martial arts historians, Chenjiagou, Wen County, Henan is the birthplace of tai chi. The various styles that have spread nowadays are derived from the style used by the Chen clan from Chenjiagou. Martial arts master Chen Wangting, who lived in late Ming and early Qing, was the founder of Chen style. On the history of tai chi development, tai chi is a unique martial arts form that took in a lot of influences across many dynasties, especially from the spearmanship of Ming martial arts masters, from swordsmanship and from the best other forms have to offer. Ming's Wang Zongyue, and Jiang Fa as well as Qing's Chen Changxing, Chen Qingping, Yang Luchan and Wu Yuxiang made great contributions to the theory, methods, development and popularization of tai chi.

词 语

  打破

融 合	**rónghé** harmonize with; be in harmony with, converge; fuse; mix

演 示	**yǎnshì** demonstrate

打 破	**dǎpò** break

shǒu tuī 首 推	first choose; first recommend	jiàn shi 见 识	knowledge
jiǎng jiě 讲 解	explain	jiū jié 纠 结	confused; to be at a loss
gè yǒu qiān qiū 各 有 千 秋	each has its own merits	yī yán wéi dìng 一 言 为 定	one word and it's settled; it's a deal; that's settled then
lǐ niàn 理 念	idea; concept; philosophy; theory	gāng róu bìng jì 刚 柔 并 济	couple strength and gentleness
fáng shēn 防 身	self-protection; defend oneself	zì wèi 自 卫	self-defense

xiū liàn 修 炼	practice austerities (Daoism) or asceticism; training
zhāo shì 招 式	movements in martial arts
gǎi biān 改 编	adapt; revise; compile
piān jī 偏 激	extreme; go to extreme
róng rù 融 入	integrate; blend; merge
sǔn shāng 损 伤	harm; damage
dà yǒu bì yì 大 有 裨 益	of great benefit; help greatly; very useful
cuò bài 挫 败	defeat

rén shì 人 士	person; figure; personage
tiān rén hé yī 天 人 合 一	heaven and man are identical; man is an integral part of nature
wàn wù 万 物	everything; all creation; all things in the universe
yì niàn 意 念	thought
cǎi yòng 采 用	adopt
bú dàng 不 当	unsuitable; improper; inappropriate
chèn qí bù bèi 趁 其 不 备	catch sb. off guard
dú dào zhī chù 独 到 之 处	distinctive qualities; specific characteristics; special; unique feature

shùn qí zì rán 顺 其 自 然	let nature take its course; take things as they come; in accordance with natural tendency
zhēng 争	fight
kàng 抗	resist; combat; fight
hú xíng 弧 形	arc; curve
gé dòu shù 格 斗 术	martial arts
chuàng shǐ rén 创 始 人	founder; originator
chuánchéng 传 承	pass on (to future generations)
wǔ guǎn 武 馆	martial arts center

wú wéi ér wéi 无 为 而 为	doing by non-doing
tí shēng 提 升	promote; upgrade
xuán 悬	lift; raise
jì lù piān 纪 录 片	documentary
fā yuán dì 发 源 地	place of origin; birthplace; source; cradle
jiā chuán 家 传	hand down from the older generations of the family; handed down in the family
kāi shè 开 设	open; set up; establish
wài zú 外 族	people not of the same clan; outsider

shī zhǎn 施　展	perform; carry out; use one's skills
dà jiāngnán běi 大 江 南 北	north and south sides of the Yangtze River; all over China
shū zhǎn 舒　展	smooth out; stretch
guà 褂	gown; robe (Chinese-style unlined garment)
jiǎn jié 简　洁	simple and clean; succinct

shùn chàng 顺　畅	smooth and unhindered; fluent
gōng bù kě mò 功 不 可 没	one's contributions cannot go unnoticed
jiān shí 坚　实	solid
hán xù 含　蓄	reserved (of a person)

专有名词

1. 太极　/ Tàijí / taiji; Supreme Ultimate (the source of all things in ancient Chinese cosmology)

2. 阴阳　/ Yīnyáng / yin and yang (the two opposing principles in nature; the former feminine and negative, the latter masculine and positive)

3. 五行　/ Wǔxíng / five elements (metal, wood, water, fire, and earth; believed by ancient Chinese to make up the physical universe, later used in traditional Chinese medicine to explain various physiological and pathological phenomena)

4. 非物质文化遗产 / fēi wùzhì wénhuà yíchǎn / intangible cultural heritage

5. 陈王廷 / Chén Wángtíng / Chen Wangting

6. 陈长兴 / Chén Chángxīng / Chen Changxing

7. 杨露禅 / Yáng Lùchán / Yang Luchan

8. 武玉襄 / Wǔ Yùxiāng / Wu Yuxiang

9. 赵堡太极拳 / Zhàobǎo tàijíquán / Zhao Bao style tai chi

10. 王宗岳 / Wáng Zōngyuè / Wang Zongyue

11. 蒋发 / Jiǎng Fā / Jiang Fa

12. 陈清平 / Chén Qīngpíng / Chen Qingping

13. 陈龙骧 / Chén lóngxiāng / Chen Longxiang

语言点

1. 以……为基础
2. 从……而来……
3. 其
4. 以……为主，由……组成……
5. ……换句话说 / 换言之，……

思 考

1. 太极拳是一项什么样的运动？

2. 传统太极拳和现代太极拳有何区别？

3. 你知道哪些太极拳套路？

4. 如果你打算学习太极拳，准备学习哪种太极拳？请说说理由。

5. 为什么说太极拳具有深刻的哲理与丰富的文化内涵？

6. 跟其他的健身运动相比，太极拳运动有哪些独特的优点？

7. 你们国家的保健养生运动有哪些？它们有什么特点？

8. 为什么说太极拳具有深刻的哲理与丰富的文化内涵？

9. 跟其他的健身运动相比，太极拳运动有哪些独特的优点？

10. 你们国家的保健养生运动有哪些？它们有什么特点？

11. 太极拳的技击特点有哪些？

12. 练习太极拳时在身体姿势上应注意什么？

13. 太极拳的借力打力是什么意思？你怎么看这个特点？

14. 填一下三种著名太极拳流派名与创始人名字：

太极拳流派	创始人、重要人物
1	
2	
3	

15. 杨露禅对太极拳的发展做了什么贡献？

16. 为什么有人把武式太极拳叫作"书生拳"和"文化拳"？

17. 你知道哪些太极拳重要的理论书？

18. 你知道中国武术史上哪些人对太极拳发展做出了巨大贡献？

第七课
Lesson 7

【 太极蓉城 】
【 Tai Chi in the City of Hibiscus (Chengdu) 】

① 休闲之都 xiūxián zhīdū
② 渊 源 yuānyuán
③ 深 厚 shēnhòu
④ 力 度 lìdù

马 兰：

乐乐，成都是中国的休闲之都，生活节奏比较慢。我猜，人们也喜欢做慢运动，练太极拳的人比较多吧？

大 萌：

你猜对了！成都打太极拳的人确实很多，而且成都人有打太极的传统。

王 乐乐：

对！成都的历史文化与太极文化渊源深厚。成都是道教发源地，道家的一些养生观对成都的文化、对成都人的生活影响是比较大的。总体来说，成都人比较喜欢自然平和、轻松舒适的事物，比较重视养生。太极拳练起来比较舒缓，既能强身健体，又能养生修性，深受成都人喜爱。

大 萌：

成都市政府对太极拳的推广力度也很大。2012 年就开始搞"太极蓉城"全民健身活动了。从成都市到 20 多个区市县都设有负责太极拳普及的组织机构，拨专款用于开展太极拳推广活动。

王乐乐:

是的。为了打造"太极蓉城",市体育局制定了专门的太极推广措施,比如在各个区不定期举办讲座,搞展示、搞比赛、推行太极进"校园"、进"企业"、进"机关"、进"写字楼"。让更多的市民了解和练习太极拳。对了,市体育局还创编了"成都太极",主要在中小学里推广。

马兰:

那现在成都大概有多少人在练太极拳呢?

王乐乐:

我记得 2015 的统计数据是 280 多万人,而且 40% 以上的是年轻人。

林川:

成都人口接近 1 600 万,那差不多六七个人中就有一个练太极拳的呀!

江一华:

难怪新闻里说成都是一座"太极之都"。

林川:

我最近还听说成都有一个"青城太极",这也是一个传统流派吧?

⑤打 造　dǎzào
⑥推 行　tuīxíng
⑦组 建　zǔjiàn
⑧乡 村　xiāngcūn
⑨氛 围　fēnwéi
⑩届　　jiè
⑪联 合　liánhé

王 乐乐：

　　对，这个流派独具道教文化特色，养生功效不错。

马 兰：

　　"青城太极"发源于青城山？

大 萌：

　　是的。它算是唯一发源于西南地区的传统太极拳流派。

马 兰：

　　哦，那我要去青城山拜师学艺。我喜欢道教文化。

王 乐乐：

　　总之，太极拳在成都普及得确实不错。现在成都主要城区都有太极拳辅导站，有的地方还有太极拳协会。成都市武术协会还组建了30多人的太极拳推广教练团，有4 000多名太极拳教学老师，向市民们义务教拳。

⑫提 升　　tíshēng
⑬包 容　　bāoróng
⑭名不虚传　míngbùxūchuán

大 萌：

据不完全统计，成都已经有 1 700 多个太极辅导和市民早晚练拳的健身点。几乎每个体育馆和公园里都有常年教练太极拳的人。

王 乐乐：

的确如此，不论是在城市还是在乡村，只要想学太极拳，出门不超过一刻钟路程，就能找到一个练习太极拳的地方。因此报上说，太极拳逐渐会成为成都人的第一运动。

大 萌：

还有一点，成都年年都要举办太极拳比赛和研讨活动。首届世界太极拳精英赛和首届世界太极拳锦标赛都是在成都举办的。

林 川：

成都太极拳氛围相当浓厚嘛！

大 萌：

是啊！2014 年成都还获得了国际武术联合会和中国国家体育总局颁发的"推广太极拳杰出贡献奖"。可以说太极健身已经成为成都的时尚潮流。

王 乐乐：

　　我看过一份"太极蓉城"全民健身活动推广的调查报告，说随着"太极蓉城普及推广，练习太极的成都人幸福感得到了大大提升"。太极和谐包容的精神已经深深融入成都的城市精神。

林 川：

　　成都作为"太极之都"，名不虚传啊！

太 极 蓉 城 · 幸 福 成 都

(Lin Chuan, Wen Xiaoxi and Ma Lan want to learn tai chi, so they came to Wang Lele's dormitory and would like him to give an overview of tai chi in Chengdu. Da Meng is also there.)

Ma Lan: Lele, Chengdu is China's leisure capital and its pace of life is slow. I guess people here also like exercising slowly, so there are probably quite a few who practice tai chi?

Da Meng: You guessed it right! There are indeed many people who practice tai chi in Chengdu. The Chengdu people have a tradition of practicing tai chi.

Wang Lele: Exactly! Chengdu's history and culture are deeply rooted in tai chi. Chengdu is the birthplace of Daoism. Some Daoist concepts of health perseverance have had relatively impact on the culture and life of the people here. In general, people in Chengdu tend to be fond of all things natural, gentle, relaxing and comfortable and stress health. Tai chi is slow and unhurried, and it not only keeps fit, but also healthy. It is loved by the Chengdu people.

Da Meng: The Chengdu government has also taken great strides in promoting tai chi. From 2012 onwards, it has promoted the "Tai Chi in the City of Hibiscus" fitness event open to the entire public. Organizations from Chengdu to more than 20 districts, cities and counties are responsible for the popularization of tai chi and allocate special funds to organize tai chi promotion events.

Wang Lele: True. In order to make "Tai Chi in the City of Hibiscus", the Municipal Sports Bureau has formulated special tai chi promotion measures, such as holding irregular lectures in various districts, organizing shows and competitions, promote tai chi to be part of schools, enterprises, institutions and office buildings. All of these are to help more people understand and practice tai chi. By the way, the Municipal Sports Bureau also compiled the "Chengdu Tai Chi", mainly for primary and secondary schools.

Ma Lan: About how many people in Chengdu practice tai chi now?

Wang Lele: As far as I recall, more than 2.8 million according to 2015 statistics, with more than 40% of practitioners being young people.

Lin Chuan: Chengdu has a population of close to 16 million people. That's about one in six or seven people practicing tai chi!

Jiang Yihua: It's no surprise that Chengdu is said to be "The City of Tai Chi" in the news.

Lin Chuan: Not so long ago I heard that"Qingcheng tai chi"can be found in Chengdu. This is also a traditional school, isn't it?

Wang Lele: It is. This school is characterized by a unique Daoist culture and boasts good health benefits.

Ma Lan: Did "Qingcheng tai chi" originate on Mt. Qingcheng?

Da Meng: It did. It's the only school of traditional tai chi that originated in the Southwest of China.

Ma Lan: Oh, well then I want to go Mt. Qingcheng to study under a master. I like Daoist culture.

Wang Lele: In short, tai chi is really popular in Chengdu. There are tai chi training stations in Chengdu's major urban areas and some place also feature tai chi associations. The Chengdu Martial Art Association has established more than 30 training groups for promoting tai chi, with more than 4,000 tai chi teachers who teach voluntarily.

Da Meng: According to incomplete numbers, Chengdu has more than 1,700 tai chi tutoring sessions and public tai chi sessions in the morning and at night. There are people who teach tai chi all year round in almost every gym and park.

Wang Lele: Indeed. Whether in the city or in the countryside, if you want to learn tai chi, you don't have to go for more than 15 minutes away from your home to find a place where you can practice. This is why newspapers say that tai chi is gradually becoming the city sport number one.

Da Meng: I want to add that Chengdu organizes tai chi tournaments and seminars every year. The first World Tai Chi Elite Competition and the first World Tai Chi Championships were both held in Chengdu.

Lin Chuan: Wow, tai chi is everywhere in Chengdu!

Da Meng: It is! Chengdu also won the "Outstanding Contribution Award for Promoting Tai Chi" awarded by the International Wushu Federation and the General Administration of Sport of China in 2014. You could say that tai chi has become Chengdu's fashion trend.

Wang Lele: I read a findings report on the "Tai Chi in the City of Hibiscus" fitness event, saying that with the promotion and popularization of said event, that the happiness of tai chi practitioners in Chengdu has greatly improved. The spirit of tai chi's harmony and inclusiveness has become one with the spirit of Chengdu citizens.

Lin Cuan: Chengdu is called "The Capital of Tai Chi" and it lives up to its reputation!

词语

乡村 xiāngcūn
village; countryside

提升 tíshēng
promote; upgrade; boost

xiū xián zhī dū 休 闲 之 都	The Capital of Leisure
shēn hòu 深 厚	deep; deep-seated
dǎ zào 打 造	create
zǔ jiàn 组 建	organize; set up; establish; form; put together (a group)
jiè 届	classifier for events, meetings, elections, sporting fixtures, years of graduation

yuān yuán 渊 源	origin; source; relationship
lì dù 力 度	strength; force; intensity
tuī xíng 推 行	carry out; put into effect
fēn wéi 氛 围	atmosphere
lián hé huì 联 合 会	federation; union; association

bāo róng 包 容	inclusive; show tolerance

míng bù xū chuán 名 不 虚 传	have a well-deserved reputation; deserve the reputation one enjoys; live up to one's reputation

专有名词

1. 蓉城 / Róngchéng / The City of Hibiscus (alternative name for Chengdu)
2. 国际武术联合会 / Guójì Wǔshù Liánhéhuì / the International Wushu Federation
3. 中国国家体育总局 / Zhōngguó Guójiā Tǐyù Zǒngjú / the General Administration of Sport of China
4. 太极蓉城 / Tàijí Róngchéng / Tai Chi in the City of Hibiscus
5. 成都太极 / Chéngdū Tàijí / Chengdu tai chi
6. 青城太极 / Qīngchéng Tàijí / Qingcheng tai chi

语言点

1. A 与 B 渊源深厚
2. 总而言之 / 总之 / 总体来说 /
3. 据……统计

思考

1. 为什么说太极拳健身会逐渐成为成都人的第一健身运动？
2. 介绍一下你们国家或你的家乡比较流行的健身运动。

第八课 【武术用语】
Lesson 8 【Martial Arts Terminology】

1. 耍花枪：

武术里面的假动作，目的是欺骗对手。后来用来比喻耍小聪明的欺骗行为。

A：刚才马老板说他要晚些时候才能还我那笔钱。

B：你不要相信他，他是在耍花枪，他的目的我清楚，就是想拿别人的钱去搞投资。

2. 十八般武艺：

中国传统武术用语，指各种兵器和武术技艺，后来常常比喻人的各种技能和本领。

A：哇！你真厉害！一个人做了这么多好吃的菜。

B：为了好好招待你们，我今天做饭时把这几年学烹饪的十八般武艺都用上了。

3. 套路：

按照一定的要求编排成套的武术动作和招式。后来也指成系统的做事方法、方式等。

1）A：这个工作我干起来有点难啊！

　　B：不着急！找到做这个工作的套路就不觉得难了。

2）A：这家商店为什么平时不打折而总是在周末打折？

　　B：周末去买东西的人多，打折会赚更多钱。这个是很多商家的套路。

3）A：昨天才去那家饭馆吃饭，你怎么又去了？

　　B：别提了，昨天老板送了一张代金券，回家发现必须两天内用完，瞬间感觉自己被套路了。

4. 花架子：

表面上好看但是非常不实用的武术动作。常比喻外表好看但缺乏实用价值的东西。

A：这个房间装修设计很漂亮啊！

B：漂亮是漂亮，就是花架子多，好看不好用啊。

5. 花拳绣腿：

好看，但是没有实际作用的假功夫。比喻只做些表面上好看、漂亮而无用的工作。

1）A：那些军人的功夫真厉害！

　　B：那当然，他们的功夫是苦练出来的，都不是花拳绣腿。

2）A：我觉得5号足球运动员的每次射门的动作都好漂亮！

　　B：是漂亮，可惜都是花拳绣腿，一个球也没踢进门。

6. 招数： 武术的动作和招式。也借用来指计策和手段。

A：我已经把所有招数都用上了，可是孩子还是哭着要买玩具。怎么办？你给支个招（数）吧。

B：我也没招（数），要不，就给孩子买吧。

7. 过招儿： 武术对手之间互相比一比本领，也用来指比赛或竞争对手之间的比拼。

1）A：你学了一年多国际象棋了。怎么样了？今天咱们俩过一下招吧。

　　B：你象棋下得那么好，我怎么敢跟你过招儿。我向你学习还差不多。

2）A：明天是哪两个队过招？

　　B：法国队和西班牙队。

8. 打太极： 指像练习太极中的太极推手一样。比喻做事情推来推去，不明确表态，含糊不说实话。

1）A：你们老板同意你的计划了吗？

　　B：别提了。每次我一问他，他就跟我打太极，一边说很支持我的计划，一边又说不好办，有难度。

2）A：你们老板说话太不直接了。
　　B：是，他总是打太极。
3）A：产品质量的问题公司应该负责吧?
　　B：谁知道呢，我去了那家公司好几次，他们总是跟我打太极，说质量不归他们管，让我去找卖家。

1. flowery of spear: Fake movement in martial arts, aims to deceive opponents. Later used metaphorically for generally deceiving behavior.

A: Ma just said that he would again need some more time to return me the money he borrowed.

B: Don't believe him; he's playing his tricks on you. I'm clear about his intentions: He just wants to take other people's money for his investments.

2. skill in wielding the 18 kinds of weapons: traditional Chinese martial arts term, using 18 kinds of weapons refers to a variety of weapons and martial arts skills, later metaphorically used to describe people with various skills and abilities.

A: Wow! You're amazing! You made these tasty dishes all by yourself!

B: In order to properly wine and dine you, I employed everything I learnt these past few years.

3. routine: Arranging martial arts actions and moves in accordance with certain requirements into a sequence. Later also used to refer to methods of doing things systematically.

1) A: Man, this job is tough!

B: Don't worry! Once you get the hang out of things, you'll find it easier.

2) A: Why does this store usually have no discounts, only on weekends?

B: Many buy groceries on weekends, which is when the shopowner can make more money with discounts. This is a pattern many businesses follow.

4. showy postures: A martial arts movement that looks good but is very impractical. Often used metaphorically to describe showy things of no practical use.

A: This room is beautifully decorated!

B: That may be the case, but it's all show with no real purpose.

5. flowery of fist with fancy footwork: Showy but impractical martial arts. Used metaphorically to describe something that is fancy but ineffectual.

1) A: The kung fu of those soldiers is really amazing!

B: Of course it is. They put a lot of hard work into their training. They're not all show.

2) A: I think that the way number 5 of this soccer team shoots the ball towards the goal is really stunning!

B: It is, but unfortunately, it's all show and no go. He didn't even score once.

6. move: movement in martial arts. Also used to refer to policies and measures.

A: I've tried everything I could think of, but my kid is crying for new toys. What should I do?

B: Nothing comes to mind. How about just buying the toys?

7. cross moves: a competition of skills between two martial arts opponents, also used to refer to matches between competitors or rivals.

1) A: You've studied chess for more than one year. Let's play a game today; how about it?

B: You excel at chess. There's no way I would play you. You teaching me would be a better idea.

2) A: Which two teams play tomorrow?

B: France and Spain.

8. do tai chi erxercises refers to something being like the pushing hands training of tai chi. Metaphor for going back and forth on a topic, not committing oneself, or being vague and not speaking the truth.

1)A: Did your boss finally agree with your plan?

B: Don't bring it up. He neither agreed nor disagreed. When I asked him, he danced around the issue. Sometimes he supports my plan, sometimes he says it's too difficult to pull off.

2)A: He's certainly nobody who says it plain.

B: Absolutely not. He's always dodging and shirking.

3)A: Who's responsible for product quality?

B: Who knows? I've been to their company many times; they're always dancing around this question. They say it's not their responsibility and I should contact the seller instead.

说一说你知道的生活中的其他武术用语。

参考文献
〔References〕

[1] 康戈武. 中国武术实用大全 [M]. 北京：中华书局，2016.

[2] 唐豪. 太极拳研究 [M]. 北京：人民体育出版社，1996.

[3] 国家体委武术研究院. 中国武术史 [M]. 北京：人民体育出版社，2003.

[4] 马虹. 陈式太极拳拳谱·拳法·拳理 [M]. 北京：北京体育大学出版社，2011.

[5] 王杰. 传统武术与现代竞技武术 [J]. 山东教育学院学报，2006（1）.

[6] 周保分. 传统武术与现代武术关系的研究 [J]. 体育世界·学术，2008（1）.

[7] 张银行. 峨眉武术的特点及发展前景研究 [J]. 四川体育科学，2008（1）.

[8] 洪奎. 对近现代中国武术概念的整理与分析 [J]. 浙江体育科学，2016（5）

[9] 李印东. 武术概念阐述 [J]. 北京体育大学学报，2008（2）.

[10] 郭玉成. 武术是融入中国传统文化的技击艺术与运动 [J]. 搏击武术科学，2010（8）.

[11] 周伟良. 武术概念新论 [J]. 南京体育学院学报，2010（2）.

[12] 赵少杰. 武术文化在对外汉语传播中的重要性 [J]. 搏击武术科学，2012（4）.

[13] 高同进. 浅析武术的功能与作用 [J]. 科技信息，2008（15）.

[14] 鄢行辉. 浅析中国传统武术对当下社会产生的作用及影响 [J]. 运动，2010(10).

[15] 郑松波. 太极拳健身原理研究 [D]. 南昌：江西师范大学，2003（6）.

[16] 徐海龙. 通过中国传统文化透视太极拳的思维方式[J]. 河北体育学院学报，2007(1).

[17] 温力. 武术的内外兼修和它的中国传统哲学基础 [J]. 体育科学，1990（3）.

[18] 太极拳：民族传统体育项目、国家级非物质文化遗产 [EB/OB].http://sports.people.com.cn/n1/2017/0712/c412605-29398908.html.

[19] 太极拳：中国文化和哲学之所在——访陈正雷 [EB/OB].http://www.sohu.com/a/157334444_457596.

[20] 蓉明年将建全民健身公共服务体系加强太极拳推广 [EB/OB].http://news.163.com/14/0326/22/9O9VETUG00014JB6.html.

附录 中国武术影视链接

[Appendix]

纪录片：《最高境界格斗术》http://travel.cntv.cn/20110802/111226.shtml/

故事片：

1.《少林寺》

2.《太极1》《太极2》

3.《太极张三丰》

4.《太极神功》

5.《少林与太极》

6.《太极》

7.《武当》

8.《太极气功》

9.《醉太极》

10.《推手》

11.《猛龙过江》

12.《龙争虎斗》

13.《精武英雄》

14.《叶问》

15.《醉拳2》

功夫电视：

1.《太极宗师》

2.《功夫状元》

3.《咏春》

4.《李小龙传奇》

5.《少林寺传奇》

武侠小说名作：

1.《笑傲江湖》金庸

2.《天龙八部》金庸

3.《射雕英雄传》金庸

4.《绝代双骄》古龙

5.《多情剑客无情剑》古龙

6.《蜀山剑奇侠》还珠楼主

7.《七剑下天山》梁羽生

8.《剑胆琴心》张恨水

Appendix: Links to Chinese Martial Arts Movies

Documentary:
The Highest Level of Martial Arts
http://travel.cntv.cn/20110802/111226.shtml/

Feature Films:
1. *The Shaolin Temple*
2. *Tai Chi1 & Tai Chi 2*
3. *The Tai-Chi Master*
4. *Tai Ji Shen Gong*
5. *Shaolin vs. Tai Chi*
6. *The Master of Tai Chi*
7. *The Undaunted Wudang*
8. *Born Invincible*
9. *Drunken Tai-Chi*
10. *Pushing Hands*
11. *The Way of the Dragon*
12. *Enter the Dragon*
13. *Fist of Legend*
14. *Yip Man*
15. *The Legend of Drunken Master*

Kung Fu TV Shows:
1. *The Tai Chi Master*
2. *Kung Fu*
3. *Wing Chun*
4. *The Legend of Bruce Le*
5. *The Legend of Shaolin Temple*

Famous Wuxia Novels:
1. *The Smiling, Proud Wanderer* by Jin Yong
2. *Demi-Gods and Semi-Devils* by Jin Yong
3. *The Legend of the Condor Heroes* by Jin Yong
4. *Two Peerless Heroes* by Gu Long
5. *Sentimental Swordsman, Ruthless Sword* by Gu Long
6. *The Gods and Demons of Zu Mountain* by Huan Zhu Lou Zhu
7. *Seven Swords of Mt. Tian* by Liang Yusheng
8. *Sword and Zither* by Zhang Henshui

图书在版编目（CIP）数据

成都印象／西南财经大学 汉语国际推广成都基地著 —成都：西南财经
大学出版社，2019.7
（走进天府系列教材）
ISBN 987-7-5504-3776-0

Ⅰ．①成… Ⅱ．①西… Ⅲ．①汉语—对外汉语教学—教材②成都—
概况 Ⅳ．①H 195.4②K 927.11
中国版本图书馆 CIP 数据核字（2018）第 241717 号

走进天府系列教材：成都印象·练武术
ZOUJIN TIANFU XILIE JIAOCAI;CHENGDU YINXIANG · LIAN WUSHU
西南财经大学 汉语国际推广成都基地 著

策　　　划：王正好　何春梅
责任编辑：李　才
装帧设计：张艳洁
插　　画：辣点设计
责任印制：朱曼丽

出版发行	西南财经大学出版社（四川省成都市光华村街55号）
网　　址	http://www.bookcj.com
电子邮件	bookcj@foxmail.com
邮政编码	610074
电　　话	028-87353785
照　　排	上海辣点广告设计咨询有限公司
印　　刷	四川新财印务有限公司
成品尺寸	170mm×240mm
印　　张	46.5
字　　数	875千字
版　　次	2019年7月第1版
印　　次	2019年7月第1次印刷
印　　数	1-2050套
书　　号	ISBN 978-7-5504-3776-0
定　　价	198.00元（套）